Are you ready to meet my grandma?

Grandma wears glasses so
that she can see.
Grandma's glasses are purple.

Grandma wears nice clothes
and gets all dressed up then
puts her glasses on.

Grandma almost always wears her glasses.
She wears them on Monday, Tuesday, Wednesday,
Thursday, Friday, Saturday and Sunday when she gets up.

She makes breakfast with them on and
dinner with them on.

Grandma's glasses don't live in a case because she always has them on. They sit on the end of her nose and on a cord.

Grandma wears her glasses as she likes to read.

Grandma wears her glasses to watch TV.
She watches the news and funny shows.

avatv

Grandma wears her glasses to go shopping.
She wears them to see the clothes to buy for Z.

DAVID JONES

Grandma goes to aqua but doesn't wear her glasses there. She jumps about in the water.

Grandma's glasses get themselves lost sometimes when grandma goes hiding from them.

Grandma cleans her glasses with warm water so that she can see out of them after they get dirty from cooking in the kitchen.

Grandma wears special sunglasses to drive the car so that she can see the road.

Granny Especial

Grandma's glasses are magic. They magnify things.
She sees everything up nice and close.

Grandma is lots of fun. She looks lovely with
her glasses on and Z always tries to grab them.

avatv

The End

www.ingramcontent.com/pod-product-compliance
Ingram Content Group UK Ltd.
Pitfield, Milton Keynes, MK11 3LW, UK
UKHW061033310726
14089UKWH00010B/227
* 9 7 8 0 6 4 5 3 3 3 3 2 9 *